Conversations Between The Sun And The Moon

Rheign

Conversations Between The Sun And The Moon
Copyright © 2023 Rheign
DARK THIRTY POETRY PUBLISHING
ISBN: 978-1-7397975-7-7

All Rights Reserved

Rheign
First edition

Artwork by Oh Jee Nam
Instagram @OhJeeNam
www.RhombiSurvivor.com

DTPP10

DARK
THIRTY
POETRY
PUBLISHING

For those seeking solace in chaos. You will get through this.

Contents

The Sun

The Moon

The Sun

Peak of Civilization

we're at the peak of civilization —
having fun
getting high and drunk.
doesn't matter where you are from
as long as you're trying to be someone.
don't know what we're doing
as long as it's something
we can call our own.
moved away from places we've outgrown
and we dream of a nonexistent place
where we work at our own pace
and smiles are a real embrace.

we're at the peak of civilization —
working hard
and getting paid in change.
doesn't matter how much we make
as long as we're proving something.
don't know where we're going
as long as it's somewhere
we can call home.
moved to a place we can flourish some
and we made it out here in space
where we smile amidst the haze
and crying for our fates.

For Eternity

they're going to bury her in a grave.
she had nothing to her name,
she had no one else to blame,
no soul to save.

matchstick burnt to the crisp.
once a flame — things were lit.
an angel tasting her first sin.
the ending is another beginning.

now she's calling for me.
sweet, sweet melancholy
resides within me,
now and for eternity.

All Girls

all girls go to hell anyways —
alluring in our devilish ways.
she's a witch
but you just call her a bitch.
you call her angel
but she feels like the devil.
she's in love
but it isn't enough.
that's why us girls cast our spells
and never take the time to dwell
on pride or shame,
men put that on us anyways.
so girls, take what you want
show off your body if you want to flaunt
it and feel beautiful and sexy in your skin.
loving your body shouldn't be a sin
but this is a man's world we're living in.

Mother Earth Beneath Me I

in the summer
one, two
we talked till we turned blue.
i danced upon the clover —
the honest greens shaping me.
three, four
the merrier the more
i felt Mother Earth beneath me —
keeping me grounded at last.
i felt like i was alive.
five, six
we can't have all that we wish —
suburbia ingrained in us.
we just want a taste of heaven.
seven, eight
starting a new slate —
celebrate the little wins.
yet, you're acting like you already won.
one, two
now my days are midnights, too —
got me begging for love.
got me feeling needy.
three, four
i saw you walk out the door
without a glance of remorse.
i submitted to survive.
five, six
no fraud love do i miss —
i'm still a crumbling mess.
know i'm never going to have a wedding.

seven, eight
i kept dropping weight
no more dandelion adventures or
piercing rays seen against the rising sun.

Pushing

dr's be pushing these pills
and making millions of dollar bills
off those barely making their bills.

dr's be pushing these pills
keeping their patients in a standstill,
keep them living for cheap thrills.

dr's be pushing these pills
prescribing the doses
and bidding goodwill.

Southern Siren I

southern siren
feel the hot Texas sun on your face
while dancing barefoot in the green grass
in your little white dress trimmed with lace
sun kissed —
summer bliss —
make a wish.
she's wild but keeps her composure —
she's a dandelion lover —
she makes you want her.
feel the cool blue water hug your waist
you swim and laugh and play
and remember your only promise is today.
fresh air —
no cares —
evil eye stare.
patchouli elixirs to return to the Elysian fields
and your love for her, signed and sealed.
little did you know, you'd soon kneel
for her.
bow down
to her.
worship
her.
she's got you wrapped around her little finger.
you never expected you'd fall for a singer —
an Edwige Feneche dead ringer.
siren by nature —
beauty in her favor —
deceit is her savior

and you can't save her.
now, you're her prisoner.

Seasons in Space

i hate when you're home.
i feel like i'm isolated —
i'm even more alone.
your mind—
your body—
baby, it's frozen.
it's so cold.
you only wanted my body to hold.
in your winters i felt the warmth —
the reflections of you unearthed.
in the spring i got scorched
by the blinding sunshine —
you said what's on your mind.
you wanted a little doll
to say yes and nod along
to play house inside
while the world turned and turned on the outside.
in the fall you'd call for me
and burn any paths you crossed —
it was all part of the plan, not a loss.
ashes all over
and you call that closure.
set me on fire
and lean into your desires.
i fall on my knees for your kerosine kisses.
i'm wishing for the burns to scar and mark
my heart so i can finally feel —
rebranding —
a fresh start.
once the dying embers lose their spark

and i've fallen apart,
i re-emerge like a shooting star —
enraged and enflamed amidst the dark.
flame and fire syzygy.
meet me at the Altar —
let's align with paradise
among the constellations in the sky.

Truth Is

truth is arbitrary.
truth is abstract.
truth is what you want to believe
and that's a fact.

Place of Be

grasping for sanity
while seeking a life of insanity.
oh momma, can't you grant me
some sort of peace and stability?

you used to hold me
and told me,
"i'll be here for you baby
when you are too close to see
the reality.
then, come to me
and we'll go to the place of Be,
where there's no anxiety,
where there's only you and me."

now, i am grown
and i need someone to hold me.
people out here selling their bones,
but they don't know
they've really sold their souls.
i feel so alone.

Maybe

maybe it's what i deserve,
maybe it's what i'm worth.
i'm not going anywhere
so just carry me up the stairs.
i don't care.
not a flying fuck anywhere.
i'm not here.
my head's up in space —
i don't want to think.

---

maybe it's what i want,
maybe it's where i belong.
i'm staying right here
and i'll carry you up the stairs.
i do care.
i'll follow you anywhere.
i'm right here,
bringing you down to earth
right next to me.

Sticks n Stones

no bumps no bruises on my arms
but there are knives in my heart.
sticks and stones may break bones
but hate and lies break my mind.
i don't know if i believe in humankind.
pushing us aside while they get high.
rising up on the hill
reach the peak —
where you smile as you kill
and we're forced to stand still
in a line —
is this really free will?

Cult Leader // Savior

every cult needs a leader,
all the saints pray for the sinners,
every gun has a trigger,
the master was once a beginner,
and the devil is a fallen angel.
she became her own underground savior —
seductress in nature.

misunderstood and cast astray
and forced to pave her own way
through the woods,
pondering the woulds, coulds, and shoulds.
then her knight in shining armor
rescued her from the world of wonder,
or so she pondered.

like lightning and thunder
he made her winters feel like summer,
till one day he did a 180
and cried that he needed saving
from his baby.

Faded Lust

once golden now rust —
i've lost the redundancy
of my consistency.
no longer vibing with the sane,
i relate more so to an alien.
things are moving yet remain unchanged,
prolonging it's willful embrace.
no longer chasing the vain —
seeking what's within my veins.
exuberant melancholy —
exhilaration between gore and glory —
but what's the real story?
one can choose to be lonely —
can't make someone be your one and only,
if you don't even hold them
or if you just want to control them.
one for the money,
two for the show,
threesome for just you, honey
and nothing else more.
my wants don't matter —
the rings of Saturn
mimic the pattern.
i never knew what true darkness was
till you walked into my life and because
of your faded lust and lack of trust,
you happily destroy
the beauty of the sun, boy.
constellations tattooed on my body
from the times you said you wanted me.

bright and unearthly —
you took pleasure in hurting me.

Red Roses II

all around flowers bloom
yet all you see is your fucking doom.
what are ya going to do?
what have you got to lose?
what are ya going to do?
you can't pick and choose.
the greener pastures on the other side
are just a masquerade — fucking lies.
are you really that surprised?
life that's just going to die.
are you really that surprised?
meet the end with unsettled goodbyes.
you need to open up,
you need to blossom, bloom
and take time for you
and give yourself room
to develop your hue
while still in your youth.
remember when those reveal
themselves to you —
that's their truth,
not the promises they unfold to you.
when you give me red roses,
i know i can't focus,
i know i can't hold this in anymore.
when you give me red roses,
they're more permanent than bruises.
i bite my teeth and get through the pain
again.
and again.

and again.
and again.
and again.

Crybaby

heaven sent face
but hell bent
on torturing me,
calling me a crybaby.

Gasping

protruding knife —
gasping for life —
i'm sorry i brought you so much strife.
i denied —
you lied —
i'm sorry that i cried.
i'm sorry i expressed emotions
when all i ever was to you was devoted.
said it wasn't just his fault in this
maybe it was i who compromised it.
i've been blinded
by other's kindness
and can seem to forgive everyone else
but can't apologize to myself.
disoriented and disassociated,
i should've been more communicative.
i compromised my free will
and worked to pay the bills
not one, not two, but three.
i gave up trying to look clean.
if i said something and you didn't like it,
i would surely be advised on it.
i wanted to sleep to escape the day —
you'd be in the other room resenting away.
it hurt you
when i said i couldn't be there to support you
as you improve and get better.
but baby, i'm as light as a feather
and soon there won't be anything left of me
but maybe that's what you wanted of me.

Mind of a Thief

nauseous
because i'm cautious
all of the time.
i've lost it.
i never said i was flawless.
i don't know what to call this.
all of those photos in your closet.
i'm living while you're sinning
and gritting your teeth.

imagine how sweet
the treat is — you leave
a garden of fruitful trees
and leaves — got a mind of a thief.
a creep, big leaps then retreat.
you don't believe me?
baby's got receipts
and records upon records to keep
and restless hours of sleep.
cheap, unclean, demean,
always has to be seen.
not a friend but a fiend.

but now
i'm washing my hands clean —
taking a step in believing in me.
finally starting to see reality.
and that my existence is not a fallacy.
no longer can you antagonize me

and this isn't the last you'll see of me.

Carnival Rides

crimson and clover — i really do love her
but i see her leaving.
she said i can't hold her down no more.
she's nauseated by the carnival rides —
over and over.
yet here we're going again and again,
her stomach turns more at every spin.
what a sick feeling it is to realize
shit's never going to change.
we once had crimson and clover
and i really did love her,
but our crimson and clover days are over.
her body is tired and can't recover
from calling me her lover —
someone that once brought a smile to her face.
oh, how she used to laugh and say,
"what a fun game it is to play.
i could do this all day."
now she's lamenting the twist and turns —
the scrambler, the zipper, and the ferris wheel —
the rides she once craved, she now spurns.
she's worn, battered, and burned —
the evidence on my hands
but i move on, unconcerned.

No Stone

no stone left unturned
and all my bridges you gladly burn.
shattered my heart of glass
since it's better to forgive than to ask.

Crimson Velvet

crimson velvet crushes my curves
as my skin kisses the sky
and bids goodbye to the sunset skies.
softer than satin —
hotter than fire —
sweeter than cherry pie —
her tender sighs are my high.
i think of her electricity day and night.
i wish i could go back and make things right.
but i'd lie if i'd say things were alright
and that i'm fine.
i still see her scarlet haze in my memories.
her presence lingers with me
as i cry to myself at night.
her blooming love dazed my mind,
now i feel like i'm dying without my lifeline.
beep beep
no separation between her and me
as much as i want to say she's moved on
i am she and she is now me.

The Ivy

blow out the smoke
to avoid feeling low.
i don't know anymore.
plastic plants —
in the wind they dance
it warmly enchants
the blue and hazy sunshine.
fluffy clouds grace
like a dream in a vase
there's no need to chase —
merely embrace.
fallen ivy in the night
used to hold me tightly,
but it lost its charm
and no longer held my arms.
i guess my ground
wasn't sound.
draped curtains
with dark resignations
and a treasure chest
of reaping benefits,
of seething regrets.
with intense dictation —
a waste of conversation
silenced by justification,
powerless in existence
and pursuant of retribution,
lacking the wont of true evolution.
a waning revolutionary,
tainting each breath

with subliminal tenderness
and disguised darkness.

Not Fallen Far

fruity ingénue
supple and sweet
believing she's just for you
but only his to consume.
not fallen far from the tree —
ripe, beautiful, and sultry.
his calloused hands and soul
cut down her whole, her core.
then he lights a match
to counteract the pain
and pointing fingers at those to blame.
he's adding fuel to the fire
to avoid the hurt and burn.
it's a full 360 turn —
he'll never learn.
her scars are earned
because she didn't learn.
he thinks he deserves
the earth to worship
his existence.
he's persistent
and hard to resist.
and she wished she didn't miss
his killer kiss.

Fool's Paradise

she's now fulfilled by a phantom of happiness.
there weren't enough evil eyes
to protect her from the prince of darkness.
rollercoaster mind twist and turns
on his island of kingdom come.
the hot sun on the white sand burns
and blisters the soles of her feet
as she happily walks along the shore
with the man who isn't there
anymore.

Rings of Life

a ring appears
within the tree
every time
the leaves change
and fall
beside the root.
things must fall
apart for new life
to grow and develop.
seedlings emerge
from the bare branches,
young birds take
their chances
with their airborne skills.
flee from the tree
they must
to expand upon
new horizons.
tree of life,
she had to survive
tumultuous storms
in order to develop
her markings.

every ring proving
her grit,
her perseverance,
her endless endurance.
three score
and in her youth evermore,

the lone ax man
approaches her core.
he cuts down her soul
without a second thought
and now she is no more.
what lingers behind
are her dead roots
and rings of life,
remnants from
her existence
and evidence of
severance.

Metamorphosis Psychosis

i feel like a shell of a soul.
am i transforming
or on the verge of a breakdown?
am i leveling up
or am i sell out?
am i breaking out of my shell
or creating my own hell?

Scary

it's scary when things change.
it's scary when things stay the same.
what's the lesser of the evils then?

Counterfeit Transmissions

i've been in survival mode for so long
i forgot what it's actually like to feel anything else.
pushed into corners and went on numerous guilt trips
that benefited others while i drowned in their oceans.
no life jackets tossed to my side just reprimands and hate
spewed from their mouths.
they're tanning on their mental yachts,
happily throwing people off who don't agree with them.
little do they know their ship is sinking and they're the
captain of their own doom.
they lifted their chins into the air without any sun care
now they're wondering why they're aging more than
those in the water.
for life is more appealing on the other side.
now they want to dive in, but they can't depart the
beloved indulgences they created.
i found my way to shore and have my toes in the sand
breathing the fresh ocean air
and walking freely among the palms
i find those who, too, nearly drowned
but found the strength within themselves to swim
onward
and overcome the tsunamis, the waves of doubt.
designed by counterfeit transmissions
and static limitations relayed so we'd forget who we are
warning us to be afraid of the depths, the darkness.
air bubbles rise to the surface as we embark,
for we need the dark to feel the light.
you willingly submerged my essence so you could claim
your height

as if followers will be at your funeral,
evidence of wrinkles and age spots appear
and they move on and forget the youth you once were.
because of your foreboding nature
i've re-emerged as a calm creature —
a witness to love as much as danger.
as you sink, i wave goodbye and say,
"see you later."

Not a Toy

i may look like a Mattel toy,
but i'm not your personal Barbie, boy.
i'm not your little gameboy
or personal Playboy.

What About Mother Mary?

smile on your face
when everything's not okay
because that's what it's like
being a fucking lady.
they point fingers and call you crazy
everyday and you just accept your fate,
but some days you question
if they could learn a lesson
from our pain, but
they don't understand what it's like
to feel the sunshine turn to rain.
they don't understand the pain
feeling sunburnt in the rain.
welcome to the beginning of the end
of civilization.
religion dictates over science these days
i don't much know much more we can take.
we're polar opposites
and we can't fix it.
what are we fighting for anyways?
our ancestors fought just so
we could see the light of day
and to pay our respects,
we play games on our phones and tablets
talking more shit than the Montagues and Capulets.
yet we're lacking communication.
they say we need Jesus
but what about Mother Mary?
she carried the holy baby
he needed her while she fed and bathed him
and was by his side when he was buried.

yet man takes all the glory,
and she's just a side character in his story.

passed down generation to generation —
if you're not a man, you embrace oppression.
you will never feel the pressure
building up inside you — life growing within you.
then tossing you aside
once you're out of your prime.
your body used and abused —
hell on earth just so you
could be alive.
no amount of myrrh and sage
could fix the human race.
it's much too late to save ourselves,
much less the world around us.
praying for better days is a foolish wish
like saying you'll go on that big trip
while counting pennies
and high off bennies.
you cant save everyone
because how could one person do it all?
it's not your call
to say we're in the age of revelations
while the world continues on its rotations
just let it go and we'll
dance in the field of clover
fuck me twice and flip me over
because that's all we can do anyways.
our souls too late to save
we're past the tipping point of saving grace.

are you going to get to heaven?
you'll have to learn some lessons.
are you going to get to heaven
if you're a god blessing digression?

Out of the Bell Jar

every time with you feels like my first
and every time with you i want you to be my last.
when i'm with you i don't think about my past.
we pass the time away from the limelight —
city lights and midnight skies.
my heart beats faster and slower
with you by my side.
i want these moments to last
as the world around us crashes
into a depression — i'm confessing
my darkest desire. you inflame my fire
to acquire my dreams which aren't irrefutable.
with you i feel beautiful.
with you i'm not as hypercritical.
i don't need an ounce of makeup on
or feel like i'm falling behind.
i can be dolled up and feel like a mess —
doesn't matter if i'm in a tight dress
or sweatpants.
your music makes me want to sing and dance,
your gaze caught me in a trance,
and i don't think i ever want to leave here.
you approach life with ease sans fear.
a gentleman from Texas with debonair.
i'm coming out of the bell jar.

at times you cradle me you tell me it's not fatal
as i'm in the fetal position.
wishing i was no longer breathing
but you got me believing in the outcome
instead of calculating the algorithms

41

in this silly little experiment under the asterisms.
what used to paralyze and tantalize
me, i learned to avert my eyes
and harden my mind like a diamond.
my tears shine and align
with my divine design.
they're not a sign of weakness
but further my completeness
of the human existence.
with you, i feel i got this.

100 Years of Growing Up

1, 2
i believed it when you said, "i love you"
3, 4
you started asking for more
5, 6
the excitement fell with each kiss
avoiding my gut instincts
7, 8
you wanted a third person to play
9, 10
you kept reminding me of the beginning
11, 12
didn't know if i'd come home to heaven or hell
what is reality or your lies, i couldn't tell
13, 14
guess our love ran out of warranty
15, 16
even though you promised it would be evergreen
17, 18
hear the garage open, my heart would be racing
running around cleaning so you wouldn't resent me
19, 20
your pleasure was making fun of me
21, 22
you took my freedom, happiness, and hope — is there
anything else you want too?
23, 24
why the fuck did i ruin my twenties — what for?
25, 26
no time for regrets or repentance, just acceptance

27,28

it's too late to change yesterday

29,30

ready for these baddie looks to be serving

while you're drinking and swerving

31,32

i used to go to the ends of the earth for you

33,34

i'm done being your little whore

35,36

you can kiss my clit

or make a run for it

37,38

it's on my time, so you can wait

39,40

time to bask in my sunshine of glory

41,42

years passed by and i'm still glamorous to you

and yet you call me the fool

43,44

it's been years since i've walked out that door

45,46

find some other bitch to suck your dick

47,48

you tried so much to get me to stay

after some years i saw right through your games

49,50

you call yourself holy while you fuck the trinity

51,52

i'm through being used by you

53,54

only my heart and coffee are shattered on the floor

the devil is elated with your rapport

55, 56

i cut my teeth on our love's remnants

57, 58

it wasn't the devil, but my soul for you to take

59, 60

find something beautiful to make it seem shitty

you'd do anything to have the blame be on me

61, 62

that was the devil's special gift to you

63, 64

anything i did was uncalled for

65, 66

there isn't a boundary you wouldn't kick

despised me when i was sick

67, 68

i now know your love was fraud and fake

69, 70

said it was you and i for eternity

71, 72

little did i know it was only going to be one who'd

make it through this lonely game for two

73, 74

now but a shell with a measly core

75, 76

you never wanted to make it this far so called it quits

77, 78

you're an adult so i'm not watching

your play-by-play day to day

79, 80

called me up and said i've been on your mind lately

81, 82

surprised you made it this far in life, boo
83, 84
told me you wanted to be gone before you had to be in
hospice dorms
85, 86
you never really wanted kids
87, 88
just wanted to pass on your name, your legacy
89, 90

anything you'd say had to be fine with me
otherwise, i'd be told off if you didn't agree
91
i used to think you were the one
92
you're just a player i see through
93
you nor can anyone claim me
i'm not a piece of goddamn property —
are we living in 1860?
94
your life's a bore and life is too beautiful to ignore
95
with you i survive, without you i'm alive
96
you were the first to call it quits but it's flipped and i'm
the bitch
97
you said only you could be my piece of heaven
98
instead you led me to hell's gate

99
day by day i was dying
while you played on with your fine dining
100

now you don't know where i am — leaving your soul in
the dust to wonder.

R2R

here's to:
reconnaissance towards a new renaissance —
revolutions towards evolution —
endings to new beginnings.

Labored with Love

honeydew, lemons, and peaches —
each her own.
lotus, lavender, and cherry blossoms
send her to the moon.
she's gotten more beautiful
as she's grown.
she's filled her fields with bountiful seeds,
labored with love till they bloomed.
she tended her days to struggles and lows,
others she celebrated her highs
and plowed the unnecessary or overgrown.
she awaits for the unveil
and doesn't force or overkill.
she's willing to wait patiently with thrill
for the new beginnings
and existing life in her field.

Life of the Party

i'm on a new vibration —
a life worth celebrating.
i'm so high
you won't even see me pass by.
i'm the life of the party,
keeping bad energies far away
from me.
i know i'm worthy of love
and high above
your minute controversies —
obstacles in my view so i'm swerving
around to get to you.
swoop, swish
pieces of me you wished you had.
but without you, i'm finally glad.

The Everglades

i dreamt of a place in the everglades
where we laughed and played all day.
we chased our dreams
till the sun went down,
then took a breath
for our hearts to calm down.
we sang,
we danced,
we created away.
the power of two in this mad place.
we weren't afraid of the pain or
how crazy life is.
in our dreams we ride
in classic lowriders.
we wandered,
we loved,
we felt our emotions.
we enjoy our own poisons
without the need of holding
it inside — we felt pride
for the first time in our life.
we set off into the ocean
without a signal or downloads
or truly knowing the destination.
everyday with you is a vacation.
we cascade the madness
with happiness.
we fucking celebrate the little things
because every now and then
we need a win.

serenity holding us as we sail off
with our blessed beloved —
the future unknown.

Our Downfall

this is our downfall
because we want it all.
i like it when you go down
and no doubt my screams
got the karen's running out of town.
they think our love is lust but
they just haven't tried enough positions
or been fucked in the right spot.
you're my gold in the rainbow's pot.
flip me over and pin me
our love isn't an i but a we.
with you i feel i can do anything.
no shame or guilt to hold me back.
you fill me up with love — not used to that.
we can ride the waves —
you're my rock and i feel safe
when i'm around you.
i don't want to remain the same
because of you.
the look you give me with your eyes
entices me to open my thighs.
i'm wrapped around you like a cobra
as we're making love on the sofa.
we dive into the covers
exploring each other's bodies all over.
feel intoxicated but i'm sober,
feel luckier than a four-leaf clover,
while pulling me closer till there is no more
space between us.

our love is out of this world.

circling round mother Venus
as she's holding her pearls.
we're dancing towards the Tropic of Cancer.
you live on a whim, i'm a planner
but i didn't anticipate you to answer
my questions. brighter than the photosphere
now we're so fucking high in the atmosphere.
divinely designed — beatus vir.
exploring the milky way on golden caps,
not knowing how much time has lapsed.
ready to take off our clothes
and ignited together we glow
as you lift me on top of you.
burning desires and our lit fused,
our bodies bright and blazing stars,
it's enigmatic but ours.
don't understand how it all started
but now i call you my dearly beloved
and i'm in love with the blessed
thing we call hope.
we devote our souls
to mother creator,
the original crusader.

I Changed Me

don't try me.
you can't buy me.
can't trust a single soul
except my own.
you saved me
but i changed me.

Roses with Thorns

take in the sunshine
and release any fears inside.
get in tune with the radiance
within your soul.
lo and behold,
a new woman unfolds.
see her now —
crown and throne,
a rose with thorns.
it's a metamorphosis —
a woman transformed.

Mother // Father

my mother is the Sun —
her light guides me to and from.
my father is the Moon —
his glow proves the beauty of light and darkness too.
my mother is the Moon —
her radiance reminds us we can't live a life through zoom.
my father is the Sun —
he shines on the possibilities of what is to come.

Evergreen Queen

pick me up, throw me down
you'll never get ahold of my crown
scream and shout, spew your doubts
you'll never rule, you fool,
four cruel words will no longer put me down.

i am the evergreen queen,
filling my kingdom with fresh opportunities.
you will see all the prosperity
from limb to limb and tree to tree,
for growth is synonymous with me
i feed on THC and leaves
to subdue earthquakes,
the never ending shakes,
and stabilize the ground
so people can hear my name,
and know to bow down.
i wear the crown
for a reason.
i rheign.
i rule.
you're just a jester,
a fool.

Nothing to Lose

where's the starry night?
take one last breath and say goodnight.
while asleep, we dream of light.
while awake, we hope of delight.

the evening swiftly approaching —
afternoon to dusk,
was once gold, now rust.

clouds and pollution
may create an illusion,
which distorts and causes confusion
since there's little to win
and nothing to lose.
words don't mean anything anyways.
the only thing we can take
to the grave is our name.

so we live as though its our last,
love like it's our first,
dance like we know the moves,
sing like we know the lyrics,
and do whatever we want to do.

Bluebonnets n Love Sonnets

lay me down in a bed of bluebonnets
i'll write about our love in sonnets.
lust makes us blind
and the world can be so unkind,
but you are
brighter than a diamond,
sweeter than wine,
a sign of the times,
more wild than flowers
that'll grow wherever it showers
and every part of you
i devour.

Lady Lazarus

she's a phoenix rising,
ascending royalty.
it's Lady Lazarus calling.
a woman on fire
with a coat of flames
and a smoke crown
and ashes are her train.
around her
a golden halo haze surrounds,
her beaming radiance.
she has men for breakfast.
she has a taste for spice
while acting all sugar and nice
and invites
new pleasures and endeavors.
she's a woman reborn
with her golden eyes ignited for more.
her wildfire confidence
is like an Aries baby dance.
she takes the rib of man
as her scepter, her stand.
she's got a macabre benevolence.
she's an American babe renaissance
in her summer awakening,
bringing the heat to the reckoning.

It's Checkmate

you call me your sweetheart,
but with every word you say,
i think your love is obsolete
in any which way.
you said you wanted a change,
a different kind of scenery,
yet you're still here,
you stayed.
you remained the exact same.
you're ready to point the blame
and add your fuel to the flames,
but i see through your games
and in this game of chess,
i hold my heart close to my chest.
i'm the queen so be blessed with my presence.
you ran with it —
your not-so-sleek gambit.
don't test me.
you'll never see the best of me
because my mind's a treasure chest
filled with unfiltered presets and unseen sunsets
and priceless doubloons you can't take
just for the sake of it —
it's not your gold to savor in.
i dove into the deep blue
to find the remnants of me and you.
images dissolving from memories
we used to crave each other like candy
but sweet turned to sour
and you preferred me when i cowered.
you wanted your "precious little flower"

to stash away in a tower,
to be admired from a distance
with no one but you to witness
my sweetness turn into darkness
you leave me to tend the kitchen
and to be your housewife living
restrained within these white walls.

and patiently waiting for your call.
you were supposed to be my knight —
to scoop me up when i was sad in the night —
but you preferred to fight
and prove you were right.
shiny reflective armor no more,
you're begging and wanting more.
no scars from war
but with a tepid tongue
your words are bullets
and your mouth a gun.
i thought you were my moon and sun
and i should have seen the warning signs,
but you took my hands and blinded my eyes —
how was i to know it was all a lie?
you said you were mine
and i wouldn't be sad or sigh
with you around because i'd
learn my lesson and end up confessing
something i didn't even do.
it was always a game to you —
there has to be a winner and a loser
your method was confusion.

circle talks on our morning walks
saying i was the lock
and you the key
and you had me believing the problem was me.
but no more crimson and clover
those days are over
i'm wiser and older,
still looking over my shoulder
but finally i can say
it's checkmate, my king
i'm done begging
and for you now,
it's game over.

The Moon

In the Yard

perfume bottles,
flawed role models,
dodging potholes,
don't know where to go.

you're living
in a prison
believing you're in heaven
when you're sitting
in a cell
baby, you're in hell.
all things given,
you're not truly living.
standing in the yard
pointing to everyone else's scars.
standing in the yard
not looking at your own heart.

beer bottles,
full time throttle,
lost control,
you can't let go.

what's your number?
step forward.
do as you're told.
you can't let go
of the chains you hold.

The Devils are Here

Will once said,
"hell is empty
the devils are here,"
though we all
walk around like
we are saints
in the making.
we're just faking
and avoiding
who we truly are —
rotten to the core.
we profusely abuse
and create wars —
sculpt, tear, rip to shreds
and forget
what our ancestors
once said,
"treat your Mother like
the royalty She is."
instead we paved over Her
and steamrolled our existence
upon Her soul.
Mother couldn't resist
our conquests
and revolutions
and now we're both losing.

Lost in Code

if you give in to the appeal,
how much of you does it reveal?

Bitches Get Stitches

she's perpetuated by the spindles of society
and threading the brokenness of femininity.
she pricks her finger to produce red
proving she isn't dead.
upon making her personality
they yell,

"too much, too little"
"too pretty, too ugly"
"too dumb, too smart"
"too ambitious, too lazy"

so she weaves the middle stitches,
along with the rest of the bitches,
following the lines,
smiling on the outside.
she pricks her fingers on the side,
already dead on the inside.

White Picket Fence Dreams

play your game,
chase the fame,
but you're going to end up playing mind games.
ride the trends,
embrace your fate,
white picket fence dreams aren't what it seems.
you've trapped yourself inside hell's gate
and you can't escape.
their sharpened ends
piercing your heart and mind.
your bloodied hands condemned
to the fenced in lifestyle,
vying for the attention of others
to prove you're worthwhile.
their wry smiles
deluding you while they revile your image.
plastic and cold is their visage
in a neighborhood of Cimmerian shade
and judgment veiled by a twilight haze.

Rectangles

rectangles in every space
where common sense is the meeting place.
fine dine and whine
where breathing is a crime
on the flip of a dime.
blinded and "fine"
taking no time to unwind.
no breaks —
emotionally confined.
time is fined
by all give and no takes —
always running but not even awake.
your youth and freedom gone in a blink,
leaving you so drained you feel you'll sink,
with no words to remove you from the brink.
we were born and raised to not think —
things are ugly till they ain't.
smiles aren't like diamonds,
a lotta fakes.
all eyes on you —
no time to break.
deeply disciplined to ignore innate
triggers and behave like life's great,
when all we feel is pressure and weight.

Southern Sirens II

southern siren
her presence like a violin
that's violent in a field of violets.
your personal corsage of riots
and you kind of like it.
your body can no longer deny it.
you can't fight it.
you succumb.
what have you become?

Voyeurs

just another voice
to the noise.
televised static
with a staged manic
under the spotlight.
the chains held tight —
just bear the pain.
one wavelength
with a slew of conversations,
only to listen
and never to be heard.
with no spoken words
to hear or heal,
yet you kneel
and worship the buzz —
you worship lust.

Screaming in Silence

happiness praises in silence,
misery cries for the masses.
all around the world
people do their dances.
some bet it all,
some never take any chances,
but pay out anyway.
some lust over lost romances —
the what ifs and could have beens.
some take cash advances
and decide to win or lose it all.
some fold and do as they're told
following everything to the book —
russian roulette is a game
strongly overlooked
by players of knowledge.
they refuse to acknowledge
Lady Fortune —
a concept so foreign
to the minds of the educated.
luck and purpose aren't as separated
as we make them out to be.
we just don't want to see the fluidity
of life, so we stifle our consciousness.
we're screaming in silence
and hiding our eyelids
from the raging fire of violets.

Essence in a Green Coat

we don't know what we're prepared for.
evil follows behind your shoulder
and you feel your body growing colder.
no time to wonder
about the bureaucratic blunders.
sauntered progress illuminated
with broken promises
that were forgotten in the wind.
mind cleansed by the immoralist
and mandated reenlistment.
they smile as they slit your throat
and embody your essence in a green coat.
you follow where they tell you to go
because you don't want to think anymore.
tension released from the trigger —
a contracted killer.
designed to ignore human emotion
and sucked you dry of any sensation.
a dead man still walking.
he used to speak silence whenever he called.
now, merely dust and pieces of a baby doll
as the only evidence of the downfall.
violence won this battle,
thanks to the leaders that herd them like cattle.

Dizzy

i can't think straight.
i don't even know my own name
and i haven't had a drop
other than the drip from the coffee pot.
i'm lost yet im at home.
i'm around others but i feel alone.
can't tell if it's the SSNRIs
or if something's in my eyes —
clouded intuition blockading,
red stoplights and the degrading.
i go go go through the motions,
ignoring the gut emotions.
through these poems i'm flowing
but the more i say the more i feel unknowing
of everything around me and my very existence.
i wish i was buried.
let flowers bloom over me.
let beauty grow upon me.
let life exist without me.
the dark side of the moon —
no matter the choice, i lose.
you refuse to admit abuse
because i didn't open up about it.
if i said things 3 times, you'd forget about it.
you'd rather be a "man" than express it.
i know you'll never confess it
and that doesn't lessen
the consequences of your deception.

Already a Believer

be my cult leader
because i'm already a believer
i never want to leave
you are the truth i finally see.
my long dark hair
waving in the air
without any fucking cares.
head hanging out the car window
with no GPS, don't have a place to go.
you speak directly to God —
you're the messenger passing it along.
it's your calling
and i've fallen
for you as my savior.
little did i know you're the traitor.
you make me want to leave.
you make me want to OD.
slippery like the snake that slithers,
your empire is withering
away yet i'm the insane
one and you speak no lies
and have done no crimes.

hallelujah hallelujah!
i love you.
i love you.
it's my time to rise up
and go to heaven.
consume the fruit juice
and i'll see you soon,

my Healer.
pour me my sweet drink
drink it like a shot.
don't want to sip
or else i might miss this.
a chance to supersede the rest of civilization
just trying to save souls
and take them to heaven.
say your prayers and blessings,
only paradise once i close my eyes.
life on earth is purgatory
with my one and only.

Trigger

i hate that bitch looking back at me.
her cold stare is triggering.
her power plays at point blank range.
her fiery rage blowing my reality out of proportion,
she's not here for any consoling.
her presence so demanding and controlling.
she needs a hole in the head
so she can finally start breathing.
lies seething from her lips
as she winks and kisses.
don't think or wince —
you have to win this standoff.
she's got all the same tricks you think of
and mirrors your every move,
acting like she's got nothing to lose
but everything to prove.
even if i destroy the portal
she'll find a wormhole
to weasel her way through.
turn the corner and there she is on cue,
like a school friend waiting for you
to spill all the dark secrets onto you.
she's loaded with envy, ambition,
and has two ears that don't listen.
she tells you over and over to quit.
this is the moment. this is it.
cock the trigger.
it's what she deserves.
feel the burn
so that soon neither of you will be of concern.

Down // Follow Me Down The Rabbit Hole

it's finally going to be okay
when i'm in a body bag.
all the pain in your life will be gone away —
your sanity can finally be safe.
no more physically feeling in a cage,
the fake stage you've been watching
will be removed from view
so you can clearly see what destruction i've done to you.
i'm an abyss of smoke
inch by inch you go down, the more you'll choke.
the façade will unfold
and you'll realize that it is my soul
that is the black hole
not the situation i'm in.
i want to protect you from any saving
before you realize what danger you're in.
you don't deserve to live in this world of hatred.
that's all i've ever known
and why i can't let go
so maybe i should embrace
what's right in front of my goddamn face.
i'm done holding this weight and chasing
happiness — a fabricated illusion i've embraced.
don't follow me down rabbit hole
for you'll lose yourself the further you go.
i suck goodness from you with my alter ego.
we know how to destroy souls
for that's all i'm good for.

Accepting Daisies

you stupid fucking bitch,
you deserve more than to burn in hell.
you don't even get a casket
just a spot in soil to rot
and bring in more life after you're gone.
even when your skin was warm
you radiated cold
with your painted black heart.
devil tattooed on you is your motto.
a malicious sinner from the start —
not even the strongest can break this bond apart
to lure and entice delicate souls in
just to rip their goodness from them
for you to indulge into.
you beg them not to come closer
so they know to avoid you
but they think they can fix you.
you just suck the light and goodness from within
others to feed your black being.
ringing in your ears, it must be time for feeding.
siren in satin, the presence appearing enlightening
but close up, she's frightening.
spectators watch from a distance
just so they can say they were there, a witness,
to the brutal images. she watches their eyes
moments before she claws them out, severing ties.
she'll tell you to leave and show the warning signs.
she doesn't lie but you take it as an invite —
she's a dead woman looking alive.
her essence is the definition of a contriving

wild mind. her smile ignites a feeling inside
your mind and you take it as real life.
thinking it's emotions
when it's just her using her magic potions
on you to feel exhilarated and liberated.
she pulls you in to keep you captivated.

i warned you the moment we met —
you said i'm a soul you'd never forget
you bet, but also a soul tainted with regrets
and more than ready to beset and test
your willingness to protect.
lone girl doesn't need saving, i'm pretending
so i can do what i do best — taking.
soft, sweet, and loving at first
once i've snatched you up, i take a turn for the worse.
long long ago i accepted daisies —
I've been them for so long i've gone crazy.
the roots weren't sustainable with my life alone
so i had to suck others in to make them grow.
i'm pushing up fucking daisies.
it's not just a phase —
death becomes me and i am she.

Black n Blue

my heart is black and blue,
matching the hues of you.
little tastes of cloud nine
so i feel as if i'm not confined.
sprinkles of my ego revived
to keep me alive
and survive.
not going to lie
some days i just want to die.
autopilot mode; "Click" vibes.
i just pass on by
while they just take their time
with my life.
no matter what i try
my eyes don't end up dry.

Ill-usion

take me back to my memories
and take me back to my daydreams.

i want to go back.
back to where it was better,
back to where everything was idyllic,
but i'd just fuck myself over
because no memories are real.
it's all a façade.
your mind plays tricks —
existence is clever
and memories are lies.
i'm sick from the elevated heights
up here on cloud nine.
altitudes altering attitudes —
breathless from the lack of oxygen
in this jurisdiction
of the highest diocese.

don't take me back to my memories
just take me back to my daydreams.

Truth Waves

when everything goes right, it feels wrong.
when everything goes wrong, it feels right.
i don't fight against the currents,
just let things pass by in blurry moments.
i'm damned by my kindness,
i'm damned by your darkness.
crash
crash
the truth comes in waves
crash
crash
and there are some storms you can't ignore.

who do you think you are?

pieces of you washing up on the shore —
you became the sea,
when you wanted to be a star.
nothing is ever enough.
ba-dum
da-dum
hear my heartbeat's rhythm
ba-dum
da-dum
in the shell of your soul.

Red Roses

you love giving me red roses
more permanent than bruises
every breath that i breathe
it's like you want me to leave
so i'll go
with a dozen roses on the floor.

your hands are a trigger
and maybe it's what i deserve
my blood on your hands .—
petals fall as i take my last dance.
this is how it ends:
one in life and one in death.

a bouquet just for me.
forever and ever, baby
no isn't a word in your vocabulary
so you made me see
how much you love me,
how much you loved me.

Tin Man

smoked myself to the oblivion.
don't have a daddy or son.
my soul taken for ransom.
where the sun don't shine,
i'm buried deep in a realm of sin
and don't know where it ends or begins
or what i'm even doing.
i've given everything from my heart and soul,
now i don't know how to feel anymore.
tin man to the core —
shallow, shiny, and nothing more.
danced on the yellow brick road,
dorothy made it home,
the great oz was all a show,
but i still have nowhere to go.
wanderlust and traveling alone,
walked till my feet got sore
and never went back once i closed that door.
all i leave with you is my heart and soul.
i don't have anything anymore
but this lone shell of a monster —
sacrificing myself for the slaughter.

Happy as a Lamb

happy as a lamb ready for the slaughter
kept in captivity, yet treat her like you caught her.
you forgot she's someone's daughter.
behind the cage, you don't see or feel her shame.
taunt, mock, and spit on her all day.
you'll say and do anything till it gets to her brain.
she's not free,
she's in captivity.
trained to behave,
trained to sit and stay,
trained to put on a show,
and to be adorned by those
wearing masks made of slate
to hide their own shame.
they act as if they're above the girl on the stage
but they, too, are educated to be patient
and joyfully watch the entertainment
with their tight collars
wrapped around their necks
waiting in line for their weekly paychecks —
the grand master production.

Catch-22

it's always a catch-22 whenever i'm with you.
i'm not over you
and no matter what i do,
it's a lose-lose.

why would you want to live the same day twice?
why would you call me your ride or die?
i don't know why.

i'm always in a catch-22 about you.
i'm over you
and no matter what i do,
it's a catch-22.

why do you refuse to cry?
why did you call me your ride or die?
you never even said goodbye.

My life's a catch-22
with or without you.
i don't know what to do
whether i'm with or without you.

Myrrh n Sage

a whirlwind craze,
amber daze,
no one to save,
no matter the amount of myrrh n sage.

pour your pretty self another drink
and drown yourself in elixirs to not think,
each drink pushing you to the brink.
the anchor tied to your ankle so you'll sink.

rising to morning regrets over last night's sunset
and slurred memories don't get to forget.
let go, let down, get rid of it.
last night was supposed to be a cool down, a reset.

Dirty Dancing

you're dirty dancing in my mind.
do you love me or just my physique?
what about me makes me unique?
prolonged silence lingers in the air.
the more you push, the further i resign.
tango on my tongue, salsa on my skin.

no rift within the sheets we're lying in.
teasing me thinking i'm one-of-a-kind.
walk around without a fucking care
in the world yet i fail and am critiqued.
not one person can fulfill what you seek
cumbia on my curves, mamba on my mind.

and keep feeding me lies time after time.

Some Bitches

some bitches bring others to life —
some bitches make others feel alive —
some bitches live just to get by —
we all fucking try.

Jungle Gym

you're the one who sits on their ass all day
and go around blaming me for living this way.
but you're scrounging for change
in the couch cushions nearly everyday
and scrolling feeds looking at the same
faces and places and gambling races
and dead ends and merry go rounds filled with strangers.
take a look at yourself in a mirror maze
nothing else is different
just more wrinkles on your face —
you haven't changed.
you're in too deep to be saved
and lost amidst the craze
you're jungle gym living
with all these saints sinning
and the evil are grinning.
i'm screaming
at myself for believing
in changing
and those say that they're willing.

In the Cell

you can't break the chains that hold you.
you won't forgive yourself for all the mistakes you've
done,
as you mark the days on the walls one by one
waiting in your cell till your time is done.
can't you tell
you're lying to yourself
and creating your own hell?
you won't break the chains that you hold.
you won't forgive yourself for all the lies you've told
and you'll be sitting in that cell till you're ice cold.

Girls with the Prettiest Eyes

girls with the prettiest eyes
have cried the most,
have heard lies the most
and expected things to turn for the worse.
those girls never put themselves first.

those girls flourish in darkness.
sitting alone in her apartment
feeling like she has to compartmentalize
her life — all it's strides and strifes.
those girls know how to be alone.
nobody's calling her on her iPhone.
she's one to seek peace and be in the zone
avoiding her own needs,
so busy she wish she had a clone.
so busy but she still feels alone.

in a crowded room — snippets of perfumes
entertained laughs encompassed by golden hues
singing tunes to herself, feeling like a lunatic.
there she goes again, assuming shit.
feeling lit, playing the bit, losing her wits —
nearly wanting to call it quits.

but she persists.
her past doesn't define her —
she's the one with the power.

Dear Demon

dear demon of mine,
keep feeding me lie after lie
as the years go by.
frame by frame direction
and scourging this hell on earth sequence.
what we do is meaningless,
nonetheless, i confess
a life without regrets,
yet many you pass will deflect
and redirect the conversation.

Serpents Elixir

words lost in translation
debating over- or under- compensation.
i'm feeling the vibrations
of my generation.
you're feeding off the venom,
consuming the income —
what have you become?

See the Sea

darling, i can't be your answer
within this sea of questions.
Existence — i know it's instinct
to be succinct with your intentions
and to move on without regrets
or a second thought
but it's hard to pretend
when you cast your shadow over sunsets.
our eyes playing with our minds —
it's too dark to see the signs.
we engage less and less over time.
the waves of change
enrage you as you see your chances
dwindle — you swindled the game,
believing you would come out on top
when you never even had a shot.
topical enhancements limit the capability
and promise of actual change —
you do these things to stay engaged,
to say you participated,
yet you remain jaded
and filled with hatred.
see the sea, baby
and ride the ripple.
feel the sea, baby
and surf the stir
because honey, you lost her
and there's no way to save her
until you surf the stormy weather
and dive into the darkness

within your own soul.

All I Want // They Show Me

all i want is the truth
while some just don't want to know.
all i want is the truth.
they say ignorance is bliss,
but how can we be alright with this?
all i want is the truth.
they loan out money to educate —
it's money they'll make and take
from the people whose lives are at stake.
to them it's just a game.
they show me their truth,
while they claim they're for the better.
they show me their truth
with the lack of respect for humankind.
use them as a warning sign.
when they show their truth
it is who they truly are
and you can't deny the scars
or when they use you as a reservoir.
they'll keep filling your pockets with hope,
then break you down and hand you the rope.

Harrowed Antidote

she took my promises as bait
and i preyed all day and night.
restless endeavors barely in sight —
pulling apart what was left of her life.
now i'm a lone wolf
starving, wanting to be full.
the moon cycle starts and
here i go again over and over.
how foolish it is to rely
on her milk and honey as my supply,
yet i'm still not satisfied.
so i go hunting in the night
and howl up to the waning crescent.
it illuminates my presence
and affirms my existence
feeling a part of my soul still missing,
so i wonder and wander while reminiscing.
phishing in the shallow water
to gain another dollar.
lying to myself with broken promises,
like how i once was Adonis
with Aphrodite as my eternal love.
provinces of gold and turtle doves
inhabit my memories —
the harrowed antidote to remedy
this immortal heartache.

Bang Bang

why you call me a lady
when i still feel like a child, a baby?
summer wine on my lips
revolutions on my hips
now revolutions pouring from my lips —
come get a kiss.
took a trip up north and it went real south.
they took away our rights,
what the fuck is that about?
nothing means fucking anything.
hipsters and politics nothing is new.
they love to hear their own voices sing
praises of their successes and all they do
and they claim to speak only of the new, the truth,
but words don't mean a damn thing.
bang. bang.
no change, no change
bang. bang.
more people to blame, to blame.
bang. bang.
more chains more chains.
bang. bang.
the people scream for change.

Maybe II

if you lie down next to me,
my hope for you is that may you simply be.
and maybe just maybe,
set your mind free
from a state of alternative realities.

i don't want to be your savior,
nor create illusions of grandeur,
but center and ground your
mind from unsettling times.
i hope you can do the same for me
if the time ever comes to be.

Falling Rock

do you know what city is near?
did it snow this same time last year?
your mountains collide on the horizon —
it feels like a little piece of heaven.
angels rest here, no beauty to compare.
you've spiked my interest
more pins than Pinterest.
you feel so far yet so near.
some are snowy skylines,
but there are no heights i fear
you compare your depths
to little hillsides and simple methods.
l'appel du vide —
danger makes you feel free.
falling rock like your need to be seen.
with breathtaking views and green sessions.
i look up and admire your stature
but to you, i was just a little creature.
you held on to me like a leech
to fulfill your needs and speed
down your foreign snow
which is not even yours and we know
you stole my soul the moment
we met — a little ghost
in your tundra of love.

i couldn't keep warm enough —
it had to be one of us.
the love dies for festivals.
i'm tired of climbing up.
your needs are satisfied,

i keep getting frostbite.
i'm turning blue.
falling rock, what else is new?
i felt like one of the fucking few who
dodged the damage and got to you,
but i'm weak and don't have a clue.
you knew the frozen power in you.
your needs were fulfilled,
i kept getting frostbit.
i feel like i've lost it.
i once was your lady of the canyon.
i once was your companion.
knees shaking like we're dancing,
felt like love everlasting
but your cold
is the only thing that's lasting.

Tidal Waves

keep fucking around to have your successor.
shoving white and pink capsules in our mouths
to keep us down
so you don't lose your crown.
you feed off others desires to fuel your empire.
you're so demanding you require
pleasure and pain to nourish your anger.
you look in the mirror and see a stranger.
what's scarier — not knowing who you are
or masquerading night after night in the bars?
if life's an illusion, you're just a façade.
you're a man who wants it all
but won't take the bet — you're afraid of the loss
and that people will see through
and toss you into the deep blue
with sharks and piranhas waiting for you.
that's just the cycle.
your movements create tidal
waves and you feel the hurricane
raging within you.
on shore, you cater
your dried fruits from your lack of labor
served on a platter from time — the waiter.
no one else to blame for your behavior
or outcomes — no singer or albums
can encapsulate the chasm
lingering within your bones.
you feel OG but you're really a clone
and you don't even know
how to atone for your vampire soul.
your goal is to drain energy.

you want to live in Beverly Hills.
do you know you lack free will
because you're designed to kill?
some things change, but you never will.
you're so icy and
it doesn't matter where you could be —
the Twin Cities or Hawaii —
you're frozen in your white tee.
your flow aligns with a Pisces
swimming against the high seas
and you don't see things clearly.
you watch your life unfold like a series
perceived as your cavalierly decisions,
you move them to align with your visions.
your exterior painted like a masterpiece
but interior designed to battle peace.
working at a faster pace
so the images don't fade.
war is always on your mind
tick tick tock
that's your freedom locked in a box.
waves consuming you from the inside out,
but somehow, you're in a drought.
head in the clouds chasing clout.
insatiable but think you're inspirational
to the rising youth.
it's scary to think that you don't have a clue
of the darkness you've fallen into.

Mother Earth Beneath Me II

one and two
i'm learning to self love.
for you, i'd never be enough —
your rage is hotter than forest fires.
three and a four
smolder your tongue on repeat.
the present coddled by your past
and distracted by others' sins.
five and six
i've finally risen
above the subliminal yields —
fruit will grow if you can wait.
seven and an eight
got a mindset like Lennon,
forever playing in strawberry fields —
a place i can imagine.
one, two, three, four
get ready boys, we're going to war.
grab your boots and your coat —
shoot your shot and stay alive.
five, six, seven, eight
hurry up and wait
choreographed patience
uniformed bodies with unarmed souls.

The Mirror Moves

i hate what i see when i look in the mirror.
i hate what i see looking back at me.
all i see are the flaws:
the pores,
the scars,
the unevenness,
the imperfections.
i see ugly,
i see worthless,
i see a piece of shit —
doesn't everyone else see this?
some scars were on accident.
some scars were on purpose.
what's the point of all this?
it's all a game anyways.
you live, you die, and rest in a yard
so why the hell shouldn't i do what i want
and reach for the fucking stars?
i can talk myself down in the mirror day after day
but every day i wake up and move
and every day i prove to myself
i can do what everyone told me i couldn't do,
and know what?
i win, they lose
because i get shit done and they watch my every move.

Galaxie Dance

i can finally see the stars tonight —
did you mean it when you said you were mine?
eclipse my heart and mind into one.
i am the moon, you are the sun.
align the stars around my head
to be a constellation for your mind
and dance with me around the galaxy.
you are my ultimate fantasy.
what's time when you have space
to explore and discover
and so much to find? — it's a wonder
how we can be lightning and thunder
and sunshine and blue skies
in another place
they turn, we turn.
they burn, we learn.
cinching Orion's Belt around my waist
and another element of you i taste,
i have to take a moment to pace
myself because all we have is space.
the stars twinkle and glow
as we tiptoe over the Big Dipper.
each eye catching moment reveals a sliver
of the burn, the fervor,
we blow things a little further.
the wind going a little farther,
winding our minds a little more
until the space and time between us is no more.

Yin Yang

she is the yin.
she is the yang
making life decisions in an instant.
most negative optimist you'll meet.
sees beauty but within herself,
beauty is nonexistent.
prayed to those above
but never gave herself any love.
she remembered her youth
and her precious time on earth —
a rebirth,
a freeing of her mind
from the cages of denial.
she now flies freely and does not look behind.
no more worries of judgment
and all its repercussions.
life seems like one paved path —
veer off and you're out of the pack,
but the lure of the human body and soul
is the innovation and creativity they show.
her shackles now gone —
a hope for each day.
she says a prayer to herself:
i am the yin.
i am the yang.
i am the sun.
i am the moon.
i have the power within myself.
to do whatever i set my mind to.
i am the beginning.
i am the ending.

i am young.
i am old.
i am wise with eagerness to learn.
i will listen but not be told what to do.

BGE

i'm entering my Bad Girl Era
and don't try to stop it.
i'm ready to flaunt it
and feel confident in my skin.
i'm ready to be flourishing
it's myself i need to be forgiving
for the hate i've been giving
towards myself, destroying my mental health.
now is my time to self reflect,
reset, and treat myself with respect
because i deserve the best
and never less.
i didn't ask for your suggestion
or your unprofessional opinion,
sometimes i just need someone to listen.
if you keep insisting,
i'm going to have to ask you to be leaving.
you don't deserve a reason
so no need for resisting —
out on your way out, darling.
i'm like a stop sign
sometimes without warning.
too late but you slam anyway
and pray no one is coming from the other ways.
you swerve and can't believe
you didn't see me coming.
i'm a woman finally becoming
and manifesting all that is for me.
my divine design aligns
with the dark and the light.

taking back what's mine:
my life.

The Dark Baptism

i'm bathing in the dark baptism of reality
and removing my lace veil.
the church bells are ringing
calling me to another dimension.
in my bathing suit, i speak my vows
to truth, my savior.
a decade of roses
around my toes
and praying for my redemption,
my resurrection.
turning my water into wine
breaking the bread of my life.
in the name of
our
mothers
daughters
and the womb of existence,
the divine feminine.

Conversations Between The Sun And The Moon is Rheign's sophomore book following her debut Empires: The Rise, The Peak, The Fall which came out in 2022. Rheign is currently based out of Dallas, Texas but was born and raised in Minnesota. From an early age, she had a passion for literature and language, with her first book written by the age of 10 and her first historical fiction novel by the age of 12. Rheign's work is inspired by 60's and 70's music, Post-Modernism, the human psyche, and true crime.

RELEASED BY DARK THIRTY POETRY

ANTHOLOGY ONE

THIS ISN'T WHY WE'RE HERE

MORTAL BEINGS

POEMS THAT WERE WRITTEN ON TRAINS BUT
WEREN'T WRITTEN ABOUT TRAINS

CLOSING SHIFT DREAMS

DESIRE

ANIMATE

THESEUS AND I

I DON'T HAVE THE WORDS FOR THIS

CONVERSATIONS BETWEEN THE SUN AND THE
MOON

www.ingramcontent.com/pod-product-compliance
Lightning Source LLC
LaVergne TN
LVHW051644080426
835511LV00016B/2477